Nita Mehta's LOW FAT Tasty Recipes

Nita Mehta

B.Sc. (Home Science), M.Sc. (Food and Nutrition), Gold Medalist

Coauthor

Rajshri

(Dietetics & Public Health Nutrition, Lady Irwin College)

SNAB
Excellence in Books

Nita Mehta's
LOW FAT
Tasty Recipes

© Copyright 2001-2009 **SNAB** Publishers Pvt Ltd

6th Print 2009
ISBN 978-81-86004-98-2

Food Styling and Photography: **SNAB** Excellence in Books

Layout and Laser Typesetting :

 National Information Technology Academy
3A/3, Asaf Ali Road
New Delhi-110002
☎ 23252948

Contributing Writers :
Anurag Mehta
Subhash Mehta

Editorial & Proofreading :
Rakesh
Ramesh

Distributed by :
THE VARIETY BOOK DEPOT
A.V.G. Bhavan, M 3 Con Circus,
New Delhi - 110 001
Tel : 23417175, 23412567; Fax : 23415335
Email: varietybookdepot@rediffmail.com

Published by :

 SNAB Excellence in Books
Publishers Pvt. Ltd.
3A/3 Asaf Ali Road,
New Delhi - 110002
Tel: 23252948, 23250091
Telefax:91-11-23250091

Editorial and Marketing office:
E-159, Greater Kailash-II, N.Delhi-48
Fax: 91-11-29225218, 29229558
Tel: 91-11-29214011, 29218727, 29218574
E-Mail: nitamehta@email.com
nitamehta@nitamehta.com
Website: http://www.nitamehta.com
Website: http://www.snabindia.com

Printed by :
DEVTECH PUBLISHERS & PRINTERS PVT LTD

Rs. 89/-

Introduction

Can you improve your chances for a healthy life by eating? Yes you can; by making the right food choices.

It has been proved by medical research that a high-fibre, low fat (only unsaturated fats) and a vegetarian diet goes a long way in maintaining a healthy lifestyle. The foods you eat provide more than nourishment and energy; the right diet can help you prevent and fight diseases. But does this mean that you have to eat bland and boiled food all the time? No way! Eat to live. Eat to improve your chances for a long and better life. Make the right food choices and cook it the right way. Cook curries by steaming the onion masala in a pressure cooker instead of the regular way of bhuno-ing (stir frying) it in oil till cooked. Almost oil free, yet delicious curries can now be cooked without a fuss!

Choosing the right spice, adding the right amount of spice and also adding the spice at the right time while cooking, is all that matters. The book presents a host of mouth watering and festive recipes for all occasions and all cooked the right way for enjoying a healthier tomorrow!

5

Contents

Food Tips for Healthy Living

- Be low on the fats and cholesterol in your diet by:
    - having toned milk
    - using *home made paneer* (cottage cheese) made from toned milk and not the *bazaar ka paneer*
    - using vegetable oils instead of saturated fats like butter, ghee, vanaspati
- Limit the intake of fast foods such as hamburgers and pizzas.
- Reduce the intake of chocolates and cream rich puddings.
- Cook mainly by baking, boiling, steaming, roasting & grilling. Avoid frying.
- Increase the intake of garlic and onions. It helps reduce cholesterol.
- Fresh lime juice with hot water is beneficial in the mornings.
- Increase use of sprouts as sprouting enhances the nutritional value manifold.
- Increase the intake of fibre in the form of raw fruits and vegetables. All fruits and vegetables that can be eaten with the skin should be taken with the skin, as apples, chikoos, cucumbers, carrots etc.

Eating Smart

- **Cereal**: Whole cereals with extra fibre are better than refined flour. *Atta, makai ka atta* & *bajra* are better than *maida*, pastas & noodles. Brown bread is better than white. When using *atta*, do not throw the *chokar* (bran) away! Unpolished rice is better than polished rice.

- **Pulses**: Preference should be given to whole or broken pulses and sprouts, they are better than *dhuli* dals.

- **Oil:** To get maximum nutritional benefit from cooking oils, use a variety of oils, because the poly unsaturated fatty acids which are lacking in one oil are present in other oils. Use of mustard oil once a week is recommended. Olive oil is believed to be the best of all the oils since it contains almost all the poly unsaturated fatty acids. By using 2-3 different oils, they supplement each other and body gets all the unsaturated fatty acids it requires to carry on the functions properly.

- **Vegetables**: Dark green leafy vegetables (*methi, saag*) contain flavinoids which protect your heart. Onions also contain flavinoids and garlic has polyphenols, so both could protect your heart.

Chatpata Protein Salad : Recipe on page 56 ➤

Eat What's Good for You

Garlic: In a recent study, a West German doctor claims that garlic may prevent heart attacks. There is proof that garlic helps break up cholesterol in the blood vessels, thus helping in the prevention of hardening of arteries which leads to high blood pressure and heart attacks.

Cruciferous Vegetables (Broccoli, Cauliflower and Cabbage): These may reduce the risk of cancer. They are rich in beta carotene and vitamins A, C and E.

Spinach: The chemical constituents of spinach are iron, vitamin A and folic acid. It is good for constipation and anaemia.

Onion: Half an onion as salad in each meal, helps thinning of the blood.

Mushrooms: These have a low fat content and are rich in vitamins and minerals. These are supposed to thin the blood and thereby prevent clotting, lower blood cholesterol.

Soyabeans: Soyabeans are a good source of lecithin which may help prevent cirrhosis of the liver. Soyabean also contain isoflavones, which show promise in liver cancer.

Capsicum: It normalizes blood pressure, improves your entire circulatory system, feeding the cell structure of arteries, veins and capillaries, as they regain elasticity. Capsicum is known to be one of the best stimulants.

Carrots: They are considered to prevent strokes and heart diseases. Juice of raw carrots is being medically recommended ever since the times of Ancient Greeks. It strengthens the heart and prevents constipation.

Apples: Special value to heart patients, they are rich in potassium and phosphorus but low in sodium. From ancient times, apple with honey is considered a very effective remedy for functional disorders of heart.

Honey: Honey is remarkable for building haemoglobin in the body. This is largely due to iron, copper and manganese contained in it. It is thus very beneficial in the treatment of anaemia. It is the best food for the heart. It is recommended in cases of arteriosclerosis (artery blockage) and of weak hearts.

Saffron: It is believed to be a blood purifier and gives appetite. It is considered a wonderful nerve and heart tonic, it is also a blood thinner.

Eating at Restaurants and Parties

- Select dishes that are steamed, baked, grilled, poached, or broiled rather than those that are pan-fried or sauteed.
- Request sauces or salad dressings 'on the side' so that you can use them more sparingly.
- Order an appetizer rather than an entree to ensure a smaller serving. If a portion is too big, eat part of it and take the rest home.
- At a salad bar, choose leafy greens, raw vegetables, beans and fruits. Avoid cheese and creamy salads. Select a reduced-calorie dressing or an oil and vinegar dressing.
- In a fast food restaurant, choose a salad without dressing, a pizza without cheese but with lots of veggies to make up for it, or a baked potato with a low-fat topping like yogurt.
- At parties or weddings, leave the gravies, pick up the solid food only.
- Don't deprive yourself of the sweet dish, choose a light one and share it with some one. Eat slowly, enjoying every bite.
- Lastly, after having enjoyed a rich meal, remember to eat very light at the next meal, may be lots of fresh fruits or a toast with some soup.

The Issue of Yo-Yo Dieting

Losing Weight & Regaining it Within Months

Whether you choose a commercial program or do it yourself, Yo-Yo dieting–losing weight only to regain it within a matter of months–is a common occurrence. A study suggested that heart disease and early death are more common among people who repeatedly lost and regained weight compared to those whose weight remained stable.

Another consequence of Yo-Yo dieting is that people who lose weight rapidly lose significant amounts of muscle tissue as well as fat. If they regain the weight, it is primarily fat, not muscle, so even if they ultimately return to their original weight, they are, in fact, "fatter" than before. What's more, this rebound weight tends to accumulate around the abdomen, which is associated with higher risks of heart disease and diabetes.

This book will help you lose weight gradually, and will help you in maintaining the lost weight. **"Eat Well and Stay Slim Forever!"**

Salt and Sugar Intake

Striking a Healthy Balance

Excess salt is poison. It drives up the blood pressure and puts an unhealthy strain on the heart. Avoid too much sugar also.

- Avoid sprinkling salt on salads or adding extra table salt to foods. Instead reach out for some lemon juice or freshly ground pepper.

- Avoid preserved and processed foods.

- Avoid adding baking soda to soften legumes and beans, like *rajmah* (kidney beans) and *channas* (chick peas).

- Try having tea and coffee without sugar or add just a pinch of sugar, rather than having artificial sweeteners.

- Select unsweetened fruit juices.

- Honey is higher in calories than sugar. 1 tbsp honey has 30% more calories than sugar does. Honey has some minerals and vitamins too whereas sugar has no nutrients your body needs, except that it provides calories.

Obesity and Diseases

Being obese increases one's risk of getting cardiovascular and other related diseases as diabetes and high blood pressure. In obese people, the calories are mainly through fats. The fats in food provide twice the number of calories provided by an equal weight of proteins or carbohydrates. One gm of fat gives 9 calories where as 1 gm of protein or carbohydrate gives nearly half the amount, just 4 calories. So keeping a check on your fat intake is very important. Do not completely remove fats from your diet as some amount of fats are required by the body for the absorption of fat soluble vitamins like vitamin A, D and E. Some fat is also required for the lubrication of the internal organs.

Morning walks and some light exercise works wonders with a balanced and controlled diet. This does not mean that one should totally avoid their favourite meals. Try to avoid fats and eat in moderation and I am positive you can do so if you include these dishes in your daily diet.

Being overweight is bad enough, but if your fat lies more in the abdomen than the hips, you are especially prone to heart diseases.

Meditation & Laughter

Laughter and meditation produce a chemical, **Endorphin**, which reduces the physical and mental stress and strengthens our immune system. This chemical is manufactured in the brain and can prevent, treat and cure many diseases without side effects.

Scientists have found out that Endorphins make the human body healthier through the production of a certain type of blood cells. These defence cells fight many diseases and are referred to as soldiers, policemen and doctors of our body.

Research showed that a laugh and smile produces $10,000 worth of Endorphins. A finding that justifies the Oriental teachings that a smile brings wealth and happiness.

When you meditate with happiness and a smiling face, you can feel the Endorphins flow all through you and a glow comes to your face. This may explain how some **prayers lead to the miraculous disappearance of disease.**

Interesting
Starters & Snacks

Whenever we think of preparing a snack, usually a fried one comes to our mind. Here I have listed some snacks which are tasty and yet not fried. They are either steamed, grilled or cooked in a very small amount of oil. These can be served as starters before a formal meal. A couple of evening snacks like unfried dahiwada and spinach upma are also included.

Stuffed Mushrooms

Serves 4

Choose big sized mushrooms so that they can be stuffed easily.

12 fresh mushrooms of a slightly bigger size
juice of ½ lemon

FILLING
½ tbsp oil
2 tbsp finely chopped onion
2 tsp cornflour
slightly less than ½ cup milk (1/3 cup approx.)
¼ tsp salt
¼ tsp pepper

1. Wash mushrooms well.
2. Boil 2 cups water in a small pan with 1 tsp salt & lemon juice.
3. Add the mushrooms. Give one boil. Remove from fire, drain & cool.
4. Gently pull out the stem, loosening from all sides of each mushroom

with the help of a knife. Discard stalks. Make a hollow in the cap with the back of a spoon. Keep mushrooms aside.

5. Mix cornflour with milk and keep aside.
6. Heat oil in a small heavy bottomed kadhai. Add chopped onion & stir on low flame for 2-3 munutes till brown. Remove from fire.
7. Add milk mixed with cornflour. Return to fire & cook, stirring till very thick. Add salt & pepper to taste. Remove filling from fire.
8. Cool the filling. Stuff each mushroom with the filling, mounting it slightly.
9. Bake in an oven at 180°C for 10 minutes in a greased oven proof glass dish.
10. Insert a tooth pick & garnish with a coriander leaf.
11. Serve hot on a bed of shredded lettuce or cabbage.

Note: Extra filling can be used as bread spread for a refreshing toasted snack.

Per Serving - Energy 40 cal, Protein 2 gm, Carbohydrate 3 gm, Fat 3 gm

Nugget Cocktail Sticks

Serves 6

Soya beans are one of the richest sources of lecithin, which are great emulsifiers of fat.

1 cup soya chunks - boiled in water till soft, keep it soaked in warm water for
½ hour - drain and squeeze
¼ cup curd (of toned milk)
1 tsp salt and ½ tsp pepper, or to taste
1½ tsp garlic paste
2 tsp oil
½ tsp ajwain
2 tbsp tomato sauce, 1 tsp soya sauce
½ tsp red chilli powder
1 onion - cut into 8 pieces and separated
1 capsicum - cut into 3/4" squares
a few tooth picks

1. Boil nuggets in water till soft. Remove from fire. Cover and keep them soaked in this water for 15-20 minutes. Squeeze and keep aside.
2. Beat curd till smooth. Add salt and pepper.
3. Marinate the nutri nugget chunks in the curd mixture. Keep aside till serving time.
4. Heat 1 tsp oil in a non stick pan. Reduce flame. Add ajwain and wait for a minute. Add garlic paste. Stir for a few seconds till it changes colour. Remove from heat. Add red chilli powder.
5. Add tomato sauce and soya sauce.
6. Return to fire. Add nuggets along with the curd mixture. Cook till almost dry.
7. Add onion and capsicum squares and saute for 2 minutes. Sprinkle some salt and pepper and mix well till dry. Remove from fire.
8. Thread a capsicum, then a piece of onion and finally a nugget on the tooth pick. Serve hot.

Per Serving - Energy 79 cal, Protein 4 gm, Carbohydrate 4 gm, Fat 5 gm

Sesame Semolina Pancakes

Serves 4-5

BATTER
½ cup thick rawa suji (coarse semolina)
¼ tsp baking powder
¼ - ½ tsp salt or to taste
½ cup curd (approx.)
1 tbsp oil - to sprinkle

TOPPING (MIX TOGETHER)
1 small onion - very finely chopped
1 small capsicum - very finely chopped
½ tomato - pulp removed and finely chopped
½ tsp salt
1 tsp til (sesame seeds)

1. Mix suji with curd to get a thick batter of a soft dropping consistency.
2. Add baking powder and salt and beat well. Keep aside for 10 minutes.
3. Add 2 tbsp water if the batter is too thick.
4. Heat a non stick tawa on low flame. Sprinkle a little oil on the tawa. Wipe it clean with a napkin.
5. Keeping the flame low, drop 3/4 tbsp of batter on the tawa to make a tiny pancake of 1" - 1½" diameter. It should not be too thin, keep it a little thick like an utthappum.
6. Drop more tbsps of batter on the tawa, keeping space between them.
7. When bubbles arise on the pancakes and the sides cook a little, sprinkle some topping mixture on all the pancakes. Press gently.
8. Put 1-2 drops of oil on each pancake.
9. Carefully over turn the pancakes to cook the other side. Press gently.
10. Cook on very low heat to cook the pancakes properly.
11. Remove the pancakes on to a plate after 3-4 minutes.
12. Serve hot for breakfast, as an evening snack or as an appetizer.

Per Serving - Energy 74 cal, Protein 2 gm, Carbohydrate 12 gm, Fat 2 gm

Chatpata Channas

Serves 3-4

1 cup kabuli channas - soaked overnight
1½ tsp oil
½ tsp sarson (mustard seeds)
1 tsp urad dal - soaked for 15 minutes
a pinch of hing (asafoetida)
a few curry leaves
½ tsp red chilli powder
2 tbsp chopped kairi (raw mango) - cut into tiny pieces or ½ tsp amchoor
2-3 green chillies - chopped
1" piece ginger - shredded
2 tsp lemon juice
2 tbsp chopped coriander

1. Drain the soaked channas. Pressure cook channas with 2 cups water & 1 tsp salt to give 1 whistle. Keep on low heat for 10-12 minutes.
2. Heat 1 tsp oil on low heat. Add sarson. When it splutters, add urad dal, hing and curry leaves. Fry for 2 minutes till dal turns brown.
3. Add red chilli powder. Add cooked channas, green chillies and ginger to it. Add salt and mango pieces. Mix well. Dry the liquid, if any, on fire.
4. Add lemon juice. Garnish with coriander leaves.
5. Serve hot or cold.

Per Serving - Energy 142 cal, Protein 2 gm, Carbohydrate 7 gm, Fat 12 gm

Spiced Button Idlis

Serves 8   *picture on facing page*

Special saanchas (moulds) which make tiny (button) idlis are available these days. Enjoy these idlis without sambhar or chutney.

1 cup suji (semolina)
1½ cups curd, approx.
3/4 tsp Eno fruit salt
2 tbsp chopped hara dhania (fresh coriander)
3/4 tsp salt

TEMPERING (CHHOWNK)
2 tsp oil
1 tsp rai (small brown mustard seeds)
½ tsp red chilli flakes or chilli powder
7-8 peppercorns - coarsely crushed
a few curry leaves

Tangy Carrot Soup : Recipe on page 51, Spiced Button Idlis ➤

1. Mix suji with curd to get a smooth batter of a soft dropping consistency. If the mixture is too thick, add some more curd.
2. Add Eno fruit salt, hara dhania and salt and mix well.
3. Immediately spoon the batter into the greased mould and steam for 14-15 minutes on medium flame till a knife inserted in it comes out clean. Cool and remove from mould and keep aside.
4. To temper the idlis, heat oil in a clean non stick kadhai or pan. Add rai and let it splutter for 1 minute. Remove from fire.
5. Add curry leaves. Add the idlis.
6. Sprinkle red chilli flakes and crushed peppercorns.
7. Return to fire. Mix well for 2-3 minutes. Serve hot.

Per Serving - Energy 75 cal, Protein 2 gm, Carbohydrate 12 gm, Fat 2 gm

Vegetables with Cucumber Dip

Serves 4

1½ cups thick curd (of toned milk) - hung in a muslin cloth for 1 hour
½ medium cucumber - peeled and grated
2-3 small flakes of garlic - crushed & chopped
½ tsp dill (soye) flakes (dried), 1 tsp lemon juice, ¼ tsp sugar, salt to taste
vegetables (carrot and cucumber) - cut into thin long fingers

1. Tie the yogurt in a muslin cloth and hang it to drain for 1 hour. 3 cups yogurt will give about 1½ cups hung yogurt.
2. Wash and grate the cucumber and drain out excess juice by pressing.
3. Combine hung yogurt, cucumber, garlic, lemon juice, dill, sugar and salt. Mix well till smooth and chill.
4. Keep the vegetable sticks in ice cold water to which some salt and lemon juice has been added, till serving time.
5. To serve, fill a glass with some crushed ice and put the sticks in it. Serve the dip along with the sticks.

Per Serving - Energy 23 cal, Protein 1 gm, Carbohydrate 1 gm, Fat 2 gm

Quick Unfried Dahivada

Serves 4-6

Prepare at least 1 hour before serving, for the bread to soak the dahi.

2 slices of fresh bread, preferably whole wheat bread
1½ cups thick curd (of toned milk) - beat till smooth
½ tsp bhuna jeera powder
½ tsp red chilli powder
1 tbsp finely chopped fresh coriander
¼ tsp kala namak
3/4 tsp salt, or to taste

CHUTNEY
1 tbsp amchoor (dry mango powder)
3 tbsp sugar
¼ tsp red chilli powder
¼ tsp garam masala
¼ tsp bhuna jeera powder
salt to taste

1. Whip curd. Mix all spices and fresh coriander to get a raita.
2. Cut sides of bread and arrange in a shallow dish.
3. Pour the dahi on it to cover completely. Let the dahi cover the empty spaces of the dish also.
4. Sprinkle red chilli powder and bhuna jeera powder on the dahi.
5. With a spoon, pour the chutney on it, in circles.
6. Garnish with bhuna jeera, red chilli powder and fresh coriander.
7. Leave in the fridge for atleast ½ hour for the bread to soak the curd.
8. Serve with extra chutney.

Note: Although these are not individual pieces of dahi badas, it tastes very much like dahi badas. I am positive you will like it!

Per Serving - Energy 34 cal, Protein 2 gm, Carbohydrate 4 gm, Fat 1 gm

Sprouty Spinach Upma

Serves 4

1 cup moong bean sprouts
4 tomatoes - remove skin by putting in hot water (blanch) & chop finely
2 green chillies - deseeded and chopped
1 cup chopped spinach
¾ cup suji (semolina)
1½ cups water
4 tsp oil
1 tsp rai (brown mustard seeds)
2 tsp salt, or to taste
½ tsp freshly ground black peppercorns
juice of ½ lemon

1. Dry roast the suji in a kadhai till it just starts to change colour and becomes fragrant. Keep aside.
2. In a clean kadhai, heat oil. Add rai.
3. When it splutters, and blanched and chopped tomatoes and green chillies. Saute for 2 minutes.
4. To this add sprouts and cook for 2 minutes.
5. Add spinach, salt and crushed peppercorns and cook for 5 minutes. Stir on low heat.
6. Add water and bring to a boil.
7. Add lemon juice.
8. Add suji, stirring continuously and cook till dry. Serve hot.

Per Serving - Energy 232 cal, Protein 9 gm, Carbohydrate 34 gm, Fat 7 gm

Broccoli Tikka

Serves 8

500 gm (2 medium heads) broccoli - cut into medium sized
florets with long stalks

1ST MARINADE
juice of 1 lemon (3-4 tsp)
3/4 tsp ajwain (carom seeds)
1 tsp salt and ½ tsp red chilli powder

2ND MARINADE
1 cup thick curd (of toned milk) - hung for 15 minutes or more
1 tsp oil
2 tsp ginger paste
½ tsp red chilli paste
3/4 tsp salt
1 tsp tandoori masala

1. Boil 5-6 cups of water in a small pan. Keep the broccoli pieces in a round stainless steel strainer (colander) over the pan of boiling water. Cover the colander with a lid and steam broccoli for 5-7 minutes till crisp-tender. Remove from fire and transfer to a clean kitchen towel. Dry the pieces well with the towel till well dried.

2. Spread the broccoli on a tray and sprinkle the ingredients of the 1st marinade. Marinate the broccoli for 15 minutes.

3. Drain the broccoli of any excess juice.

4. Mix all the ingredients of the 2nd marinade in a large pan. Add the broccoli to it and mix well. Check the salt and add more if needed. Keep in the refrigerator till the time of serving.

5. Rub the grill of the oven or tandoor with some oil. Heat a gas oven and grill for 10 minutes or grill in a preheated electric oven at 210°C/410°F only for 10 minutes. Do not over grill it, it turns too dry. Serve hot.

Per Serving - Energy 60 cal, Protein 4 gm, Carbohydrate 5 gm, Fat 3 gm

Grilled Curd Cheese Fingers

Serves 4-5   *picture on facing page*

1 cup thick curd (prepared from toned milk) - hung for 1-2 hours
3-4 tbsp cabbage - shredded, 2-3 tbsp carrot - grated
1 green chilli - deseeded and finely chopped
salt and pepper to taste
2 tbsp green mint or coriander chutney
6 slices bread, preferably brown bread

1. Beat hung curd in a bowl till smooth.
2. Add cabbage, carrot, green chilli, salt & pepper. Mix well. Add a little extra salt, otherwise the fingers taste bland.
3. Spread the curd mix generously on a slice.
4. Spread some chutney on another slice. Place the chutney slice, with the chutney side down on the curd slice. Press well.
5. Grill in a sandwich toaster or in the oven on the wire rack till browned.
6. Cut into 4 fingers and serve hot. Repeat with the other 4 slices.

Per Serving - Energy 84 cal, Protein 3 gm, Carbohydrate 16 gm, Fat 1 gm

Steamed Baby Corns

Serves 6   *picture on page 2*

200 gm baby corns
1 tbsp green coriander paste made by crushing a few leaves
½ cup dahi (of toned milk)
1½ tsp garlic paste, 2 green chillies - deseeded and chopped finely
1 tsp salt, or to taste, a pinch of haldi
some chaat masala - to sprinkle

1. Pressure cook all ingredients together, except the chaat masala, to give 1 whistle. Remove from fire.
2. After the pressure drops, open the cooker and dry the water.
3. Serve sprinkled with some chaat masala.

Note: If baby corns are not available, cut the regular corn into 1Ω" pieces and pressure cook to give 1 whistle and then keep on low flame for 8-10 minutes. Choose tender corns.

Per Serving - Energy 47 cal, Protein 2 gm, Carbohydrate 8 gm, Fat 1 gm

Minty Strawberry Dip

Serves 8

3 cups curd (of toned milk) - hung in a muslin cloth for 1 hour
3/4 cup chopped strawberries
¼ cup chopped mint
¼ tsp sugar, salt to taste

TO SERVE WITH
vegetable sticks of carrots, cucumber or blanched broccoli florets

1. Tie the yogurt in a muslin cloth and hang it to drain for 1 hour. 3 cups yogurt will give about 1½ cups hung yogurt.
2. Blend strawberries for a few seconds to make a strawberry puree.
3. Beat the yogurt till smooth.
4. Mix strawberry puree, mint, salt & sugar to the beaten yogurt. Chill.
5. Serve with peeled carrot and cucumber cut into sticks and blanched broccoli florets with long stalks.

Per Serving - Energy 25 cal, Protein 1 gm, Carbohydrate 2 gm, Fat 2 gm

Sesame Potato Fingers

Serves 6

4 slices of brown bread
1 tsp kale til (black sesame seeds), or white sesame seeds

MIX TOGETHER
2 boiled potatoes - grated, 1 tsp tomato sauce
1 green chilli - deseeded and finely chopped
2 tbsp chopped hara dhania (fresh coriander)
½ onion - very finely chopped, ½ tomato - very finely chopped
3/4 tsp salt, ¼ tsp pepper and ½ tsp chat masala, or to taste

1. Press some potato mix on the bread.
2. Sprinkle some sesame seeds. Grill in an oven till the toast turns crisp.
3. Cut each slice into 3 long fingers and serve hot.

Note: For children, you may put a slice of cheese on the potatoes and sprinkle with sesame seeds. Grill and serve.

Per Serving - Energy 64 cal, Protein 2 gm, Carbohydrate 15 gm, Fat 0 gm

Healthy Soups

The recipe of my favourite soup is to collect some assorted vegetables available at home in the refrigerator and boil them in some water along with 1-2 tomatoes and 2 tbsp of split pink lentils (dhuli masoor ki dal) which adds to the nutrition also besides the taste. I like to add a few peppercorns too. Vegetables like a floret of cauliflower, 1 carrot, 4-5 mushrooms or a cup of chopped spinach makes a great combination. In summers you may add ghiya also when too many vegetables are not available. Cook till vegetables turn tender. Remove from fire and cool. Churn in a blender and strain. Add salt to taste and serve piping hot.

Lemony Lentil Soup

Serves 10-12

1 cup pink lentils (dhuli masoor ki dal)
8 cups water
1" piece ginger - chopped
10-12 saboot kali mirch (peppercorns)
1 potato - peeled and very finely diced
2 tsp oil
¼ cup chopped coriander
¼ tsp hing
2 tsp salt, or to taste
½ tsp black pepper
½ tsp jeera (cumin) powder
juice of 1 lemon, or to taste

1. Rinse lentils. Pressure cook lentils with water, ginger and saboot kali mirch to give one whistle. Keep on low flame for 2 minutes. Remove from fire. Cool. Grind to a puree in a blender.
2. In a separate non-stick pan, heat oil. Add hing. Wait for a few seconds. Add very finely chopped potatoes. Fry for 2 minutes.
3. Add lentil broth. Add more water if required to get the right consistency.
4. Add salt, pepper, fresh coriander and lemon juice. Cook for 10 minutes on low flame, till potatoes turn soft.
5. Serve hot garnished with coriander.

Per Serving - Energy 49 cal, Protein 3 gm, Carbohydrate 7 gm, Fat 1 gm

Dal & Tomato Rasam

Serves 4

4 large tomatoes - chopped roughly
2 tbsp arhar dal (pigeon peas)
1½ tsp salt, or to taste

TADKA, BAGHAR (TEMPERING)
1 tsp oil
a pinch of hing (asafoetida)
½ tsp jeera (cumin), ½ tsp rai (brown mustard)
few curry patta

RASAM POWDER
Dry roast these ingredients. Cool and grind to make rasam powder.
Store the excess.

1 tsp jeera (cumin seeds), 1 tsp saboot dhania (coriander seeds)
3-4 dry, red chillies
½ tsp saboot kali mirch (peppercorns)
2 tsp channa dal (split Bengal gram)

1. Wash and cut tomatoes roughly.
2. Wash dal. Add arhar dal, tomatoes and salt. Add 4½ cups water and boil for 15-20 minutes on low medium flame till dal is done.
3. Remove from fire and strain. Mash the tomatoes well while straining.
4. To the liquid, add 2-3 tsp of rasam powder and give 2-3 boils. Keep aside.
5. For tadka, heat a teaspoon of oil. Add hing, after a few seconds add jeera, mustard and curry patta.
6. When jeera turns golden, add the oil to the rasam. Serve hot.

Per Serving - Energy 30 cal, Protein 1 gm, Carbohydrate 3 gm, Fat 1 gm

Herbed Green Pea Soup

Delicious soup without a drop of oil!

Serves 6   *Picture on page 2*

2 cups shelled peas
2 medium potatoes - chopped
1 onion - chopped
1" piece ginger - chopped
1" stick dalchini (cinnamon)
1 tsp jeera (cumin seeds)
1 tbsp mint leaves
1 cup chopped spinach
1 tbsp coriander
salt to taste, ½ tsp pepper, or to taste
5 cups water
1½ cups toned milk

1. Cut potatoes and onions into small pieces. Grate the ginger.
2. Boil peas, potatoes, onion, ginger, dalchini and jeera with 5 cups of water in a pan.
3. When they are almost cooked, add spinach, mint and coriander. Cook uncovered for 3-4 minutes till the spinach turns tender.
4. Remove from fire. Strain, reserving the liquid.
5. Cool the unstrained vegetables and grind in a blender with a little liquid. Mix with the reserved liquid. Pass the soup through a sieve.
6. Add milk to the soup. Mix well. Boil. Add salt and pepper to taste. Serve piping hot.

Per Serving - Energy 78 cal, Protein 5 gm, Carbohydrate 14 gm, Fat 0 gm

Lauki and Tomato Soup

Serves 4

½ kg tomatoes - roughly chopped
250 gms (1 small) lauki or ghiya (bottle gourd) - peeled and chopped
½" piece ginger, 6-8 saboot kali mirch (peppercorns), 1 onion - chopped
1½ tsp salt, ½ tsp pepper, or to taste, a pinch of sugar
fresh coriander to garnish
a dash of butter (optional)

1. In a pressure cooker, boil the tomatoes, ghiya, ginger, saboot kali mirch and onion with 4 cups of water to give 1 whistle. Keep on low flame for 4-5 minutes. Remove from fire.
2. Cool and puree in a blender. Strain the puree. Boil soup. Add the sugar, salt and pepper. Add a dash of butter. Add fresh coriander.
3. Simmer for a few minutes. Serve hot.

Note: For variation, instead of ghiya one may use 2 tbsp of moong dhuli dal and juice of half a lemon.

Per Serving - Energy 42 cal, Protein 2 gm, Carbohydrate 8 gm, Fat 0 gm

Tangy Carrot Soup

Serves 4   *picture on page 29*

2 big (250 gms) carrots - peeled and chopped
1 potato - peeled and chopped
1 tsp oil
1 onion - chopped, 8-10 peppercorns, 1" piece ginger - chopped
4 cups vegetable stock or water
juice of one orange or 1/3 cup ready made orange juice
3/4 tsp salt, or to taste & pepper, 2 tbsp chopped coriander

1. Saute onion, peppercorns and ginger in 1 tsp oil in a non stick pan till onions start to change colour.
2. To it add carrots and potato. Stir for 2-3 minutes on low flame. Add water. Bring to a boil. Simmer on low flame for 10-15 minutes till the vegetables get cooked. Remove from fire.
3. Cool and grind to a puree in a blender. Strain the vegetable puree.
4. Add orange juice, coriander, salt & pepper. Boil. Serve hot or cold.

Per Serving - Energy 66 cal, Protein 1 gm, Carbohydrate 12 gm, Fat 1 gm

Hot 'n Sour Vegetable Soup

Serves 4

1 tsp oil
1 cup grated cabbage
½ cup grated carrots
1 tsp soya sauce, 2 tsp chilli sauce
½ tsp salt, ½ tsp pepper, or to taste
4 cups vegetable stock or water
3 tbsp cornflour - dissolved in ½ cup water
¼-½ cup paneer - finely diced, 2 tbsp lemon juice

1. In a pan, heat oil. Add carrot and cabbage. Stir for a minute.
2. Add soya sauce, chilli sauce, salt and pepper. Add 4 cups water.
3. Boil. Dissolve cornflour in ½ cup water, stir well and add the cornflour paste into the soup. Stir till it boils. Remove when the thick.
4. Add some more cornflour dissolved in water, if the soup appears thin. Add tiny cubes of paneer. Add lemon juice and serve hot.

Per Serving - Energy 57 cal, Protein 3 gm, Carbohydrate 4 gm, Fat 3 gm

Tomato Soup with Rice and Basil

Serves 8

2 tsp oil
1 onion - finely chopped
4 tsp cornflour, 1½ cups toned milk
750 gms (8 large) tomatoes - chopped, 2 tbsp tomato puree (ready made)
1" stick dalchini (cinnamon)
2 tbsp fresh basil leaves (tulsi) - chopped or 2 tsp dried basil
2 tsp salt, ½ tsp freshly ground pepper, or to taste, 2 tbsp cooked rice

1. In a pan saute the onion in 2 tsp oil till soft.
2. Reduce heat. Stir in cornflour. Add milk, tomatoes, tomato puree, cinnamon, basil, salt and pepper. Boil. Cover and cook till tomatoes turn soft. Remove from fire. Cool.
3. Pour the soup in a blender and blend to a puree. Strain the soup.
4. Add 3 cups water to the soup and give 2-3 quick boils.
5. Serve hot garnished with some cooked rice and fresh basil leaves.

Per Serving - Energy 36 cal, Protein 2 gm, Carbohydrate 3 gm, Fat 1 gm

Paalak ka Soup

Serves 4-5

3 cups chopped spinach (paalak)
3 cups water, 1 tej patta (bay leaf)
¼" piece ginger - chopped, 1-2 flakes garlic
1 cup toned milk
salt & pepper to taste, 1 tsp lemon juice

GARNISHING
½ cup grated or mashed paneer, prepared from skimmed milk

1. Boil chopped spinach with bay leaf, garlic, ginger and 3 cups water. Cover and simmer for 7-8 minutes. Cool. Puree in a blender & sieve.
2. Add salt & pepper to taste. Boil the spinach puree for 2-3 minutes.
3. Add milk, stirring continuously. Boil again. Keep aside.
4. To serve, boil soup. Remove from fire. Add lemon juice, stirring continuously. Garnish with grated or mashed paneer and serve.

Per Serving - Energy 38 cal, Protein 3 gm, Carbohydrate 4 gm, Fat 1 gm

Lite Salads

Fresh vegetables should be cut and kept in ice cold water for about an hour to make them crisp. Slices of cucumber, onion rings, leaves of lettuce and radish chunks look and taste great when kept in chilled water. These should be pat dried on a clean kitchen towel before adding the dressing. However, tomato slices and fruits should be cut fresh and tossed in the dressing immediately. The dressing should not be added too much in advance as it makes the salad limp.

Chat-Pata Protein Salad

Serves 6   *picture on page 11*

½ cup kabuli channa (chick peas) - soaked overnight
½ cup rajmah (kidney beans) - soaked overnight
½ cup moong sprouts
1 capsicum - cut into half and then into thin rings
1 tomato - cut into half and then into round slices
1 onion - cut into half and then into thin rings
½ or a small cucumber - cut into thin slices

DRESSING
1 tsp salt
1 tsp pepper
1 tsp ajwain (carom seeds)
1 tsp amchoor
a few basil leaves
4 tsp vinegar or lemon juice
2 tsp oil

1. Soak rajmah and channas together. Next morning discard water. Add 1 tsp salt and pressure cook with 2 cups water to give 2 whistles. Keep on low flame for 10 minutes. When the pressure drops, strain the rajmah and channas and discard the water. Keep aside.
2. Steam the moong sprouts by placing them on a strainer or colander over a pan of boiling water for 3-4 minutes. Cover the colander while steaming. Remove from fire and keep aside.
3. Put all the dressing ingredients in a bottle and tightly close the cap. Shake vigorously to mix well. Keep aside.
4. Keep the cooked rajmah, channas, sprouts, capsicum, onion, tomato and cucumber in a large bowl. Chill.
5. An hour before serving, pour the dressing over and toss well with two forks to mix well. Serve.

Per Serving - Energy 135 cal, Protein 7 gm, Carbohydrate 20 gm, Fat 3 gm

Tomato Balls

Serves 6

6 tomatoes - medium sized, even shaped and firm
2 tbsp channa dal - cooked
100 gms paneer (of toned milk) - grated
1 small apple - peeled & finely diced, 1 tsp mustard paste
½ tsp salt, 8-10 peppercorns - crushed, a few coriander leaves

1. Boil channa dal in some water with ½ tsp salt. Cook till just done. Strain and keep aside.
2. Cut tomatoes from top. Scoop the pulp. If you wish, rub a pinch of salt inside the hollow tomatoes. Keep them inverted on a plate.
3. Mix dal, paneer & apple. Add mustard paste, salt & pepper to taste.
4. Fill the mixture in tomatoes. To make the tomatoes stand upright, cut a thin slice from the base of the tomatoes.
5. At serving time, bake at 200°C for 12-15 minutes till soft but firm.
6. Garnish each with a coriander leaf. Serve on a bed of cabbage leaves.

Per Serving - Energy 29 cal, Protein 1 gm, Carbohydrate 4 gm, Fat 1 gm

Vegetable Sticks with Paneer Dip

Serves 6

home made paneer prepared from ½ kg of toned milk
1 cup curd - hung for ½ hour
2-3 flakes garlic, 2 tbsp chopped coriander leaves
juice of 1 lemon , a pinch of sugar, ½ tsp salt, ½ tsp pepper
½ onion - very finely chopped

VEGETABLE STICKS
carrot, cucumber, tomato, radish

1. In a blender, mix paneer, curd, garlic & coriander leaves to a paste.
2. To this add sugar, lemon juice, salt & pepper and mix well.
3. Add very finely chopped onion. Mix well.
4. Cut the carrot, cucumber, radish and tomatoes longitudinally into long fingers or sticks.
5. Arrange the salad in a plate with the dip in the centre.

Per Serving - Energy 19 cal, Protein 1 gm, Carbohydrate 1 gm, Fat 1 gm

Fruity Salad in Orange Dressing

Serves 4

½ cup cabbage - chopped
½ cup carrot - chopped
¼ cup onion - chopped
½ cup tomatoes - chopped
½ cup grapes or strawberries - halved or chopped
½ cup orange segments

ORANGE DRESSING
1 tbsp oil
¼ cup orange juice (fresh or ready made)
1 tsp lemon juice
2-3 flakes garlic - crushed
½ tsp oregano
½ tsp salt and pepper, or to taste

1. Mix all fruits and vegetables in a large bowl. Chill.
2. Mix all ingredients of the orange dressing in a bottle. Close cap and shake well to mix. Keep aside.
3. An hour before serving, pour the dressing over the fruit and vegetable mixture in the bowl.
4. Toss lightly with two forks. Add more salt and pepper if desired.
5. Refrigerate till serving time.

Per Serving - Energy 37 cal, Protein 0 gm, Carbohydrate 5 gm, Fat 2 gm

Low Calorie Creamy Salad

Serves 6

2½ cups toned milk
½ cup curd or juice of ½ lemon - to curdle milk
1 cup thick curd - hung for ½ hour, 2 tsp sugar, few drops vanilla essence
½ carrot - finely cubed and boiled till crisp tender
½ capsicum - cut into thin strips, ½ cup grapes -halved
1 apple - chopped without peeling, ½ cup chopped cucumber (kheera)

1. Boil milk. Reduce flame and add curd or lemon juice to curdle the milk. As soon as the milk curdles, remove from flame and strain through a muslin cloth. Leave it in the cloth for at least ½ hour till the water (whey) gets drained.
2. Blend paneer, curd, sugar and essence in a blender.
3. Remove from blender to a bowl. Add salt and pepper. Mix most of the fruits and vegetables in the curd-paneer mixture, keeping aside some for garnishing. Transfer to a serving bowl. Chill. Serve.

Per Serving - Energy 61 cal, Protein 3 gm, Carbohydrate 8 gm, Fat 1 gm

Low Fat Main Dishes

No more frightening curries! Oily and rich curries are no longer desirable. An interesting way of preparing curries is by steaming the onion masala without oil in a pressure cooker instead of bhuno-ing it in a kadhai with oil.

This section includes recipes of vegetables which have a low fat content (low hidden fat) such as spinach, mushrooms, tindas, carrots, etc. Very little amout of oil has been added, so cook the vegetables on low heat and prefereably in non stick utensil. Healthy foods, such as recipes with soya bean, are also included.

Basil Tomato Paneer

Serves 6   *picture on facing page*

300 gm paneer (of toned milk)
4 large tomatoes - blanched, peeled & pureed
1 tbsp oil
1 large onion - chopped finely
8 laung (cloves) - crushed
10-12 saboot kali mirch (peppercorns) - crushed coarsely

MARINADE
1½ cups curd
2 tsp cornflour
a few basil leaves - finely chopped (2 tbsp)
1½-2 tsp salt
3/4 tsp red chilli powder

OTHER INGREDIENTS
2-3 tsp tomato ketchup, 1 tsp butter
1 tsp tandoori masala

1. Cut paneer into 1 inch pieces.
2. Mix all ingredients of the marinade and marinate the paneer it.
3. Blanch the tomatoes in boiling hot water for a few minutes. Remove its peel and grind to a puree in the blender.
4. In a pan heat oil. Add the onions add laung. Stir fry for a few minutes till the onions turn light brown.
5. Add the prepared tomato puree tomato ketchup, butter and tandoori masala. Cook for 5-7 minutes till absolutely dry. Remove from fire and let it cool. Keep aside till serving time.
6. At serving time, add the marinated paneer with all the curd to the tomato-onion masala. Cook on low heat for a few minutes till you get the desired gravy. Do not over cook. (The curd might curdle if the heat is too high or if the gravy is kept for too long on fire.)
7. Transfer to a serving dish. Sprinkle with crushed peppercorns. Garnish with chopped basil leaves.

Per Serving - Energy 69 cal, Protein 3 gm, Carbohydrate 3 gm, Fat 5 gm

Mushroom Jalfrazie

Serves 4

200 gms mushrooms - cut into thick slices
1 tbsp oil, ½ tsp ajwain (carom seeds)
1½ onions - finely chopped, 3-4 flakes garlic - crushed
1 green chilli - finely chopped, 1" piece ginger - shredded
2 tomatoes - blanched, peeled & finely chopped, 1 tbsp tomato ketchup
¼ tsp red chilli powder, 1 tsp salt, or to taste
1 capsicum - cut into thin long strips

1. Wash the mushrooms and cut into slices.
2. Heat oil. Reduce heat and add ajwain. Add onions & cook till golden.
3. Add garlic. Stir for 2 min. Add tomatoes, tomato sauce, green chillies and ginger. Cook on low flame till tomatoes turn dry (8-10 minutes).
4. Add mushrooms, salt & red chilli powder. Cook till mushrooms get cooked. Keep mushrooms spread out while they are being cooked.
5. Add capsicums and cook for 2-3 minutes. Serve.

Per Serving - Energy 62 cal, Protein 2 gm, Carbohydrate 6 gm, Fat 3 gm

Tinda Tandoori

Serves 4

½ kg tinda - medium size
½ tsp haldi, salt to taste
2 tsp oil
½ tsp jeera (cumin seeds)
2" piece cabbage - shredded (½ cup)
½ cup peas - boiled
2 boiled potatoes
¾ tsp amchoor
½ tsp red chilli powder, ¾ tsp salt, ½ tsp garam masala
1 tsp tandoori masala
1 tsp kishmish (raisins) - optional
1 green chilli - deseeded and chopped

1. Peel the tindas. Scoop them.
2. Add ½ tsp haldi and 1½ tsp salt to 4 cups water. Add tindas to the boiling water and cook till just done.
3. For stuffing: In a kadhai, heat 2 tsp oil. Add ½ tsp jeera, let it turn golden. Add a pinch of haldi. Mix and add shredded cabbage. Stir fry for a while and remove from fire.
4. To the cabbage, add boiled peas, mashed potatoes, salt, red chillies and amchoor. Add raisins and green chillies. Mix well.
5. Brush the outside of the tindas with a little oil.
6. Fill the stuffing in tindas, heaping it a little.
7. Bake for 15-20 minutes in a moderate oven at 200°C and serve hot.

Per Serving - Energy 113 cal, Protein 5 gm, Carbohydrate 17 gm, Fat 3 gm

Baby Corn & Paneer Delight

Serves 6

200 gm paneer (of toned milk) - cut into 1½" long fingers
200 gm baby corns - cut into pieces length ways
1 small red & 1 small green capsicum - cut into long strips
1 onion - chopped
2-3 green chillies - deseeded and chopped
6-8 garlic flakes - crushed
1" piece ginger - cut into juliennes (match sticks)
1½ tsp salt, or to taste
1 tsp red chilli powder
4 tbsp tomato puree
½ tsp sugar
1 tsp soya sauce
2 tbsp oil
1 tsp saboot dhania (coriander seeds)
½ tsp ajwain (carom seeds)

1. Cut paneer into 1½" long fingers.
2. Cut the baby corn longitudinally into half. Boil water with a pinch of haldi and some salt. Add baby corns. Boil. Cook for 2-3 minutes till crisp-tender.
3. Heat 1 tbsp oil in a kadhai. Add the babycorns, spread them out in the kadhai. Do not overlap. Cook till brown specs appear. Remove from oil.
4. In a clean kadhai, heat 1 tbsp oil. Reduce heat and saute onions, garlic, ginger and green chillies, till onions turn brown.
5. Add ajwain and dhania saboot. Stir for a few seconds on low flame.
6. Add tomato puree, sugar and soya sauce.
7. Add 3-4 tbsp water and simmer for a minute.
8. Add the bell pepper, cut into strips. Stir fry for a minute.
9. Add baby corns and paneer. Add salt and red chilli powder.
10. Mix well and serve hot.

Per Serving - Energy 84 cal, Protein 3 gm, Carbohydrate 7 gm, Fat 5 gm

Baked Potatoes with Spinach

Serves 4-6

400 gm (4 large) potatoes
½ kg (1 bundle) spinach - blanched and ground to a paste
1¼ cups toned milk
1 tsp salt
½ tsp pepper
a pinch of jaiphal powder (ground nutmeg)
1 onion - finely chopped
5-6 flakes garlic - crushed
2 tsp oil
20 gm (1 cube) cheese - grated, optional
a small bunch of fresh coriander - finely chopped
6-8 saboot kali mirch (peppercorns) - crushed

1. Peel and cut potatoes into ¼" thick round slices.
2. In a pan boil milk with salt, pepper and jaiphal. Add the potatoes in milk and cook covered on low flame till potatoes get done. Remove from fire when they get cooked. Remove the potato slices from the milk and keep aside. Keep aside the left over milk also.
3. In a pan stir fry onions till soft, add garlic and cook till onions turn light brown. Keep onions aside.
4. Boil some water in a pan and add spinach to it. Boil uncovered for 3-4 minutes till the spinach turns soft. Strain and cool. Grind it in a blender to a paste.
5. Add the spinach puree to the leftover milk of potatoes. Cook it for a few minutes till the excess liquid dries.
6. To assemble, in a greased dish set the cooked paalak at the base.
7. Then place a layer of cooked potatoes over it.
8. Spread the onion garlic layer. Grate some cheese over it if desired. Sprinkle with crushed peppercorns and coriander.
9. At the time of serving, bake for 20 minutes at 180°C.

Per Serving - Energy 128 cal, Protein 5 gm, Carbohydrate 20 gm, Fat 3 gm

Chholia Curry - Almost Oil Free

(kale channe soaked overnight & boiled, can be prepared in the same way)

Serves 4　　　　*picture on facing page*

1 potato - cut into 8 pieces
1 cup chholia or hare channe (fresh green gram)
1 tsp oil
2 tomatoes - ground to a puree
1 tsp dhania powder (ground coriander)
½ tsp each of garam masala and red chilli powder
¼ tsp each of amchoor and haldi, salt to taste
2 green chillies
2-3 tbsp chopped green coriander

GRIND TOGETHER
2 onions
1" piece ginger, 3-4 flakes garlic
3-4 laung (cloves)
seeds of 2 moti illaichi (brown cardamoms)

1. Grind onions, ginger, garlic, laung and seeds of moti illaichi to a paste with 2 tbsp water. Put in a pressure cooker without any oil and pressure cook to give 2 whistles. Remove from fire.
2. When the pressure drops, add 1 tsp oil. Add all masalas - dhania powder, garam masala, red chilli powder, amchoor and haldi. Stir for 2 minutes on low flame.
3. Add the freshly prepared tomato puree and cook for 8-10 minutes, till dry.
4. Add aloo, chholia, chopped coriander, whole green chillies and salt. Bhuno for 3-4 minutes.
5. Add enough water to get a gravy of the desired consistency and give 2 whistles. Serve hot garnished with tomato wedges.

Per Serving - Energy 158 cal, Protein 9 gm, Carbohydrate 24 gm, Fat 3 gm

Vegetable Masala

Serves 4

2½ cups chopped mixed vegetables - 1 carrot, ½ cup peas, ½ cup chopped
beans, ½ of a small cauliflower - cut into small florets
3 medium onions - ground to a paste
1½ tbsp oil, 1 tsp jeera (cumin seeds)
3/4 tsp red chilli powder, 1 tsp salt, or to taste
2 tsp besan (gram flour), 1 tsp lemon juice

1. Cut vegetables into ½" cubes and boil till crisp-tender or microwave
   on high for 4 minutes. (Do not over cook)
2. Dry roast the besan till it turns fragrant. (Gives out a roasted smell).
3. Heat oil in a non stick kadhai, add jeera to it. Let it turn golden.
4. Add the onion paste and fry till it turns golden brown.
5. Add the boiled vegetables. Add salt & red chillies. Cook for 2 minutes.
6. Add besan. Cover and cook the vegetables on low heat for 5 min.
7. Remove from fire. Add lemon juice while serving.

Per Serving - Energy 81 cal, Protein 1 gm, Carbohydrate 10 gm, Fat 4 gm

Spinach Nugget Kadhi

Serves 6

1½ cups soya nugget chunks
2 cups curd (of toned milk)
½ cup besan (gram flour)
5-6 cups water
1 cup finely chopped spinach - made into a paste in grinder
1½ tsp salt, or to taste
¾ tsp red chilli powder

TADKA (TEMPERING)
1 tbsp oil
a pinch of hing (asafoetida)
1 tsp jeera (cumin seeds)
3-4 dry, whole red chillies
a pinch of red chilli powder
1 tbsp kasoori methi (dry fenugreek leaves)

1. Boil nuggets in salted water till soft. Remove from fire. Cover and keep aside for 10-15 minutes till very soft. Squeeze gently and keep aside.
2. Heat 1 tbsp oil in a nonstick kadhai or pan and saute the nuggets in oil till well browned. Keep aside.
3. Mix besan and curd well to make a smooth paste. To it add 5 cups of water.
4. Wash the spinach well and grind it into a fine paste in a blender.
5. Add salt, chilli powder and spinach to the besan-curd mixture. Transfer to a big, heavy bottomed pan. Boil and then cook for 10-15 minutes on low flame.
6. Add the nuggets to the curd besan mixture and cook the kadhi again on low flame for another 10 minutes.
7. **For tadka:** Heat oil, add jeera & hing. When jeera turns brown, add the whole, red chillies. Remove from fire. Mix and add red chilli powder and kasoori methi. Mix for a second. Pour it on the kadhi. Serve hot with rice.

Per Serving - Energy 142 cal, Protein 11 gm, Carbohydrate 8 gm, Fat 8 gm

Kesari Channa Dal

Serves 4

1 cup channa dal
¼ tsp haldi, 1 tsp salt
½ cup toned milk
4-5 strands of kesar (saffron)
1 onion - sliced
a pinch of jaiphal powder (ground nutmeg)

MASALA PASTE
1 tbsp oil
1 onion - chopped
2 tbsp mint leaves, 2 tbsp fresh coriander leaves
2 green chillies - chopped
2-3 laung (cloves), 2-3 saboot kali mirch (black peppercorns)
4-5 cashew nuts
2 tsp khus khus (poppy seeds)
1" piece ginger - chopped
2-3 flakes garlic - chopped

1. Pressure cook channa dal in 3 cups water with ¼ tsp haldi and 1 tsp salt to give 2 whistles. Reduce flame and cook on low flame for 5 minutes.
2. Soak kesar in hot milk and keep aside.
3. To prepare the masala paste, heat 1 tbsp oil and add onions. Stir fry till brown. Add all the other ingredients of the masala paste and fry for 2-3 minutes more. Remove from fire. Cool. Grind to a paste with the kesar milk to a paste.
4. Heat 1 tbsp oil and add the sliced onion. Stir fry till brown.
5. Add the paste and stir fry the paste for 1 minute.
6. Add the channa dal along with the water in it.
7. Mix well. Cook for a few minutes.
8. Serve sprinkled with fresh coriander and ground nutmeg.

Per Serving - Energy 144 cal, Protein 7 gm, Carbohydrate 19 gm, Fat 4 gm

Baked Greens Topped with Corn

Serves 6　　　　*picture on back cover*

1 cup spinach - shredded
1 cup cabbage - shredded
1 cup broccoli - finely chopped (finely chop 1" of the stalks also)
½ cup boiled or tinned corn kernels
½ tsp red chilli flakes
4-5 flakes garlic - crushed
1 onion - thinly sliced
8-10 peppercorns - crushed coarsely
1 tbsp oil
1 tomato - cut into slices
some mint leaves - to garnish

SAUCE
1½ tbsp oil
2 tbsp atta
1½ cups toned milk
1 tsp salt and ½ tsp pepper, or to taste

1. Boil water in a large pan with 1 tsp salt. Add broccoli. Add other greens after 1 minute. When the boil comes again remove from fire. Strain well to drain water.
2. Heat 1 tbsp oil. Saute garlic and onion till onion turns transparent.
3. Add crushed peppercorns and ½ tsp salt.
4. Squeeze greens gently and add to the onions. Cook till dry on low flame for 3-4 minutes. Remove from fire.
5. To prepare the sauce, heat oil. Reduce heat and add atta. Cook for 1 minute. Add milk, stirring continuously. Stir on medium flame till a sauce of medium thick consistency is obtained. Add salt and freshly ground peppercorns to taste. Keep aside.
6. In a dish arrange the greens 1½ - 2" thick layer.
7. Spread cooked corn (not too much) on it.
8. Sprinkle some red chilli flakes.
9. Pour the prepared sauce to cover well.
10. Arrange slices of tomatoes on it. Bake at 200°C for 25-30 minutes or till golden brown. Garnish with mint leaves.

Per Serving - Energy 100 cal, Protein 4 gm, Carbohydrate 9 gm, Fat 5 gm

Soyabean Palak

Serves 4 *picture on facing page*

½ bundle spinach - chopped (3 cups), ½ cup soyabeans - soaked overnight
2 onions - sliced, 2-3 flakes garlic - crushed
½ tsp dhania powder, ½ tsp red chilli powder, ¼ tsp haldi, salt to taste
2 tomatoes - chopped, 1 tbsp tomato sauce
2-3 green chillies, 1" piece ginger - cut into matchsticks
2 tbsp oil, ½ tsp jeera, a pinch of hing

1. Pressure cook soya beans with 3/4 cup water and ½ tsp salt to give one whistle. Keep on low flame for 10 minutes. Remove from fire.
2. Heat oil. Add hing. Add jeera. When it turns golden, add onions.
3. Cook till transparent. Add garlic. Stir for a minute. Add masalas.
4. Add tomatoes and tomato sauce. Cook for 2 minutes.
5. Add boiled soyabeans. Cook covered for 5-7 minutes on low heat.
6. Add spinach. Cook uncovered for 10 minutes on high flame till dry.
7. Add green chillies and ginger. Stir and serve hot.

Per Serving - Energy 164 cal, Protein 10 gm, Carbohydrate 10 gm, Fat 9 gm

Sirke Waale Mushrooms

Serves 2-3   *picture on cover*

200 gm mushrooms - each cut into half
2 spring onions - chop the white part finely and the greens into 1" pieces
2 tsp oil, 3-4 flakes garlic - crushed
½ tsp red chilli paste, 2 tbsp tomato puree, 1 tsp tomato sauce
2 tbsp vinegar
½ tsp peppercorns - crushed to a coarse powder, 3/4 tsp salt, or to taste

1. Wash the mushrooms carefully and trim the stalks. Cut each mushroom into half or into 4 if they are big.
2. Heat a non stick pan with 2 tsp oil. Reduce heat. Add garlic and chopped white part of spring onions. Stir till onions turn transparent.
3. Add chilli paste, tomato puree, tomato sauce and vinegar. Stir.
4. Add the mushrooms. Sprinkle peppercorns and salt. Cook uncovered over low heat for 7-10 minutes.
5. Add the greens of spring onions and stir for Ω minute. Serve.

Per Serving - Energy 59 cal, Protein 2 gm, Carbohydrate 3 gm, Fat 4 gm

Ajwaini Broccoli

Serves 2

250 gm (1 small flower) broccoli - cut into medium florets with 1½" stalks
½ tbsp oil
1 tsp crushed garlic
1 tsp ajwain (carom seeds)
1-2 tsp lemon juice
½ tsp salt, or to taste

1. Steam the broccoli in a steamer/covered sieve over a pan of boiling water for 5 minutes. The broccoli should retain its colour and remain crunchy. Keep aside.
2. At serving time, heat oil in a non stick pan and add the ajwain. Reduce heat. Wait for a few seconds. Add garlic paste. Saute over a low flame till it just changes colour.
3. Add the broccoli and salt. Saute for 5 minutes.
4. Sprinkle with lemon juice and serve immediately as a side dish.

Per Serving - Energy 105 cal, Protein 7 gm, Carbohydrate 10 gm, Fat 4 gm

Kesari Dahi Waale Aloo

Serves 4   *picture on cover*

250 gm, about 15 baby potatoes or 4 regular potatoes - boiled and peeled

MIX TOGETHER
1¼ cups curd
2 tsp cornflour, 3/4 tsp salt
¼ tsp kesar (saffron) dissolved in 1 tbsp hot water
2 tbsp chopped (mint) - chopped, 2 tbsp dhania (coriander) - chopped

OTHER INGREDIENTS
1 tbsp oil
½ tsp shah jeera (black cumin), 1 moti illiachi, 2-3 laung (cloves)
1 onion - sliced
2 tbsp ginger garlic past
½ tbsp red chilli powder, ¼ tsp haldi, ½ tsp salt
1 tsp dhania powder, ½ tsp garam masala
2 green chillies- slit deseeded & cut into thin long pieces
1 tomato - cut into 8 long pieces

1. Boil and peel potatoes. If the potatoes are the normal ones, cut them into four pieces. If using baby potatoes, keep them whole.
2. Beat curd to make it smooth. Add all ingredients given under mix together, with the whipped curd.
3. Heat oil in a fairly large kadhai. Add shah jeera, moti illaichi & laung. Wait for 1 minute.
4. Add onion. Stir fry till golden brown on low heat.
5. Add ginger-garlic paste. Mix.
6. Add red chilli powder, haldi, salt, garam masala & dhania powder.
7. Add potatoes and mix well. Keep them spaced out in the kadhai, do not overlap them. Stir very occasionally, scraping the masala which sticks to the bottom. Stir occasionally for 8-10 minutes till crisp.
8. Add the curd mixture. Cook on low heat till the masala dries up and turns a little thick and coats the potatoes.
9. Add green chillies & tomato. Remove from fire. Serve.

Per Serving - Energy 138 cal, Protein 4 gm, Carbohydrate 24 gm, Fat 4 gm

Sukhe Matar Paneer with Kasoori Methi

Serves 4

250 gms paneer (of toned milk) - cut into small cubes
1½ cups shelled peas
1 tsp jeera (cumin seeds)
¾ tsp red chilli powder, 1½ tsp salt, or to taste
½ cup kasoori methi (dry fenugreek leaves)
1 tbsp oil
1 tsp amchoor, ½ tsp garam masala

1. In a kadhai, heat oil and add jeera. Let jeera turn golden brown.
2. Add peas to it and stir fry for 2 minutes on low flame. Cover the kadhai with the lid for few minutes. Cook till peas are done.
3. Add cubed paneer, salt, red chilli powder to it and stir well. Cook for 2 minutes.
4. Sprinkle kasoori methi, amchoor and garam masala. Cook on low flame for 5 minutes. Serve hot.

Per Serving - Energy 91 cal, Protein 5 gm, Carbohydrate 6 gm, Fat 5 gm

Baked Baingan ka Bharta

Serves 4

1 large round baingan - roasted on a gas flame
1 onion - finely chopped, ½" piece ginger - chopped finely
2 tomatoes - finely chopped
2 green chillies - finely chopped
½ tsp red chilli powder, ½ tsp garam masala, ¼ tsp amchoor
1½ tsp salt, or to taste, ½ tsp bhuna jeera
1 tsp oil (optional)
2 tbsp chopped hara dhania for garnishing

1. Rub a little oil over the baingan and roast over a gas flame until the skin gets charred and starts to peel off and the flesh is soft.
2. Remove the charred skin of baingan. Wash and mash the flesh with a fork. Mix all ingredients with baingans in a large oven proof dish.
3. Preheat the oven at 200°C. Bake the bharta in a shallow ovenproof dish for 40 minutes, stirring in between. Serve hot with chappatis.

Per Serving - Energy 26 cal, Protein 1 gm, Carbohydrate 5 gm, Fat 0 gm

Matar Curry in Steamed Onion Masala

Serves 4

1 potato - cut into 8 pieces, 3/4 cup shelled peas, 1 tsp oil
2 tomatoes - ground to a puree, 1 tsp dhania powder (ground coriander)
½ tsp each of garam masala and red chilli powder
¼ tsp each of amchoor and haldi, salt to taste
2-3 tbsp chopped green coriander for garnishing
2 onions, 1" piece ginger, 1 green chilli, 1 tsp jeera - grind all together

1. Grind onions, ginger, green chilli and cumin seeds to a paste with 2 tbsp water. Put in a pressure cooker without any oil and pressure cook to give 2 whistles. Remove from fire.

2. When the pressure drops, add 1 tsp oil. Add all masalas - dhania powder, garam masala, red chilli powder, amchoor and haldi. Stir for 2 minutes on low flame. Add the fresh tomato puree.

3. Cook for 8-10 minutes, till dry. Add aloo matar, salt and bhuno for 3-4 minutes. Add 2 cups water and give 1 whistle. Keep on low flame for 2-3 minutes. Serve hot garnished with chopped coriander.

Per Serving - Energy 67 cal, Protein 2 gm, Carbohydrate 11 gm, Fat 1 gm

Low Calorie Sweets

Have a sweet tooth? No problem! I have created these special recipes to keep you and your family fit.

Hung curd is whipped and some toned milk is added to it to make the mock cream for the family favourite chocolate souffle. A kheer with cabbage may sound uninteresting but my family loves this mysterious kheer! It keeps them in shape, healthy and without being deprived of a sweet dish after the meal.

Yogurt Chocolate Souffle

Serves 6   *picture on facing page*

2 cups toned milk, 2 tbsp cornflour, 2 tbsp cocoa, 9 tbsp sugar
3/4 cup thick curd (of toned milk) - hung for ½ hour and squeezed well
2 tsp gelatine, 1½ tsp vanilla essence, ½ tsp butter, fresh fruits to garnish

1. Dissolve cornflour and cocoa in ¼ cup warm milk.
2. Keep the rest of the milk on fire. When it starts boiling, add the dissolved cornflour and cocoa, stirring continuously. Add the sugar also. Cook, stirring till the milk turns slightly thick, like custard and coats the spoon. Remove from fire. Mix in butter. Keep chocolate custard aside.
3. Sprinkle gelatine on ¼ cup water kept in a small pan. Keep on low flame till gelatine dissolves. Remove from fire and add to the chocolate custard.
4. Whip the hung curd till smooth. Put in a cup and add enough milk, (about ¼ cup milk) to make upto 3/4 cup. Add essense also.
5. Add the curd mix to the cooled custard and mix well. Transfer to a serving dish and keep in the fridge till set. Garnish with fruit & mint.

Per Serving - Energy 79 cal, Protein 2 gm, Carbohydrate 13 gm, Fat 2 gm

Orange Cake with Orange Sauce

Serves 15   *picture on page 1*

Just 2 eggs are used to prepare a big cake, right for 15 people. The orange juice if fresh is naturally healthier, but ready made juice will also do!

1¾ cups maida (plain flour), 1½ tsp baking powder
1 cup orange juice, 1/3 cup oil
1¼ cups powdered sugar, 2 eggs
¼ tsp dalchini (cinnamon powder), ½ tsp vanilla essence
4-6 almonds - cut into fine pieces, 1-2 tbsp brown sugar

SYRUP
½ cup orange juice, 3 tbsp honey, 1 tbsp cornflour

1. To prepare the cake, sift maida with baking powder.
2. Beat eggs till stiff in a clean, dry pan.
3. Add sugar gradually and beat well till frothy.
4. Add oil, little at a time and keep beating.
5. Add orange juice, cinnamon powder and vanilla essence.

6. Add ½ of the maida and mix gently. Add the left over maida too.
7. Transfer to a greased ring mould, (a jelly mould with a hole in the centre.) Sprinkle brown sugar and almonds on top.
8. Bake at 180°C for 30-35 minutes. Bake till a knife inserted in it comes out clean. Cool and remove from dish. Keep aside.
9. Mix all ingredients of the syrup and cook till it attains a coating consistency.
10. Transfer the cake to a serving dish. Prick lightly. Pour the syrup over the cake. Serve.

Note: When you use ready made orange juice, 1 small pack of ready made orange juice (Tropicana) is enough for the cake and the sauce also. If you wish, you may make extra sauce and serve in a sauce boat along with the cake.

Per Serving - Energy 110 cal, Protein 2 gm, Carbohydrate 19 gm, Fat 3 gm

Hide 'n Seek Pudding

Serves 8

1 packet (100 gm) plain chocolate biscuits (Kellogs Chocos)
some chocolate sauce (ready made)

VANILLA SPONGE CAKE
2 large eggs - separate yolk and white
5 tbsp powdered sugar
5 tbsp maida (plain flour)
1 tsp baking powder, 1 tsp vanilla essence

CUSTARD SAUCE
½ kg (2½ cups) toned milk
3 tbsp custard powder, 3 tbsp sugar, ½ tsp vanilla essence

1. To prepare the cake, grease a loaf shaped cake tin. Sift maida with baking powder. Keep aside. In a clean, dry pan beat egg whites till stiff. Add sugar gradually, beating after each addition. When all the sugar has been used, add the egg yolks. Fold in the maida with a wooden spoon, moving the spoon upwards and then downwards

(fold) to mix in the maida. When the maida is well mixed, transfer to the greased tin and bake at 200°C for 12-15 minutes. Remove from the oven after 5 minutes. Cut into thin fingers and keep aside.

2. To prepare the custard, dissolve the custard powder in a little milk. Boil the rest of the milk and add the custard paste when the milk boils. Cook on low heat till it turns slightly thick. Add sugar and cook for a few minutes till sugar dissolves. Remove from fire. Add essence.

3. Break all biscuits roughly, each biscuit into 6-8 pieces, (small pieces). Keep aside.

4. To assemble the dessert, in a medium size serving dish arrange a layer of sponge fingers. Soak them with some hot custard.

5. Sprinkle half the biscuits on it, to cover.

6. Again arrange a layer of sponge fingers.

7. Pour custard to cover completely. Chill. Sprinkle remaining biscuits.

8. Squeeze some chocolate sauce in a design over it, may be continuous diagonal lines, or in circles. Serve chilled.

Per Serving - Energy 151 cal, Protein 5 gm, Carbohydrate 15 gm, Fat 4 gm

Baked Apple Dessert

Serves 4

4 apples - cut into four, peeled and sliced thinly
3 tsp castor sugar
½ tsp cinnamon (dalchini) powder
1 tbsp custard powder
8 marie biscuits - crushed coarsely

1. Cook the apples with sugar, cinnamon powder, and ¼ cup of water over low heat in an open pan, for about 15 minutes, until excess liquid dries up. Leave to cool.
2. Mix together the marie biscuits and the custard powder with the apple mixture.
3. Transfer to an oven proof serving dish. Place in a hot oven at 200°C for 15 minutes.
4. Serve immediately accompanied with custard.

Per Serving - Energy 63 cal, Protein 0 gm, Carbohydrate 15 gm, Fat 0 gm

Ginger Fruit Salad

Serves 4

2 red apples - cut into small pieces without peeling
2 oranges
½ cup green grapes
½ cup black grapes
2 bananas - cut into round slices
½ cup gingerale
1 tbsp lemon juice
a few mint leaves - chopped

1. Core and dice the apples but do not peel them.
2. Peel oranges and divide into segments, discarding all the white pith.
3. Put all the fruits in a serving bowl and add the gingerale. Toss gently and leave in the refrigerator for 30 minutes for marination.
4. Garnish with mint leaves and serve in individual bowls or glasses.

Per Serving - Energy 75 cal, Protein 1 gm, Carbohydrate 17 gm, Fat 0 gm

Ghee Free Gajar ka Halwa

Serves 4

½ kg carrots - grated thickly
¼ cup sugar
2 cups toned milk
½ tsp green cardamom powder
2 almonds - thinly sliced, for garnishing

1. Grate the carrots.
2. Put the carrots and milk in the pressure cooker. Pressure cook till the pressure builds up and the whistle is about to come. Do not let the whistle come. Reduce heat and keep on low flame for 8-10 minutes. Remove from fire.
3. After the pressure drops, open the cooker and cook till the milk dries.
4. Add sugar and cardamom powder. Cook till it turns dry again.
5. Transfer to a serving bowl. Garnish with thinly sliced almonds.

Per Serving - Energy 120 cal, Protein 4 gm, Carbohydrate 23 gm, Fat 0 gm

Cabbage Kheer

Serves 4-5

1 kg toned milk
2 cups grated cabbage - finely grated
1/3 cup sugar, or slightly less
½ tsp chhoti illaichi (green cardamom) powder
1 tbsp kishmish (raisins)
2 tsp cornflour - dissolved in ¼ cup milk
2-3 almonds or pistas - chopped

1. Cook cabbage with milk in a kadhai till it turns slightly thick.
2. Add sugar and cornflour paste. Cook till it turns thick like kheer.
3. Add cardamom powder and cook for a few minutes.
4. Serve hot or cold garnished with some chopped almonds or pistas.

Per Serving - Energy 100 cal, Protein 6 gm, Carbohydrate 14 gm, Fat 0 gm

BEST SELLERS BY SNAB
Excellence in Books

101 Paneer Recipes

101 Vegetarian Recipes

SPECIAL Vegetarian Recipes

Cakes & Cake Decorations

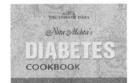

DIABETES Cookbook

Burgers & Sandwiches

Vegetarian MUGHLAI

CHOCOLATE Cookbook